JUMPING CROSS-COUNTRY FENCES

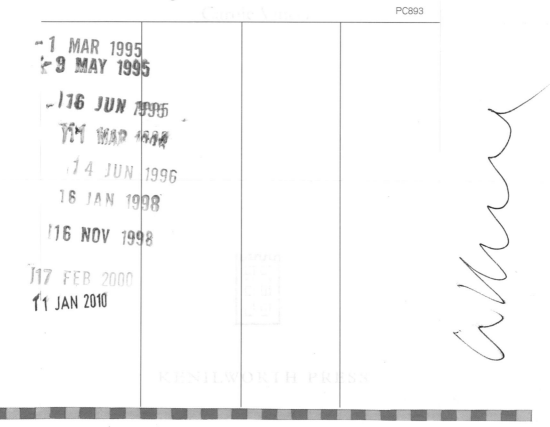

First published in Great Britain by
The Kenilworth Press Limited,
Addington, Buckingham, MK18 2JR

© The Kenilworth Press Limited 1991

Reprinted 1992, 1994

British Library Cataloguing in Publication Data
A catalogue record for this book is available from the British Library.

ISBN 1-872082-07-6

Typeset by DP Photosetting, Aylesbury, Bucks

Printed in Great Britain by Westway Offset, Wembley

CONTENTS

JUMPING
CROSS-COUNTRY FENCES

4 Introduction
5 Tack and equipment
6 Rider's protection and safety
6 Walking the course
7 The start and the first fence
8 Ditch away
8 Steeplechase fence
9 Triple bar
9 Sharks' teeth
10 Trakehner
11 Bullfinch
11 Open ditch
12 Coffin
14 Water fences
15 Open water or ditch
16 Steps and banks
17 Sunken road
18 Drop fence
19 Hayrack with a false groundline
20 Combination fences
21 Bounce fence
22 Corner
23 Jumping into darkness
24 Final thoughts

Introduction

Safe and successful cross-country performances depend upon the thorough training of horse and rider. Confidence and experience build up slowly, but confidence is easily destroyed.

Before attempting any cross-country, the rider must have mastered the basics of riding on the flat and over fences with a good safe position, and the horse must be fit and well schooled.

The rider must be in control *at all times*. Reckless riding has no place on a cross-country course and is in fact dangerous.

When cross-country schooling, always take someone experienced who can help and advise. Check the take-offs and landings of unknown fences, and watch for hidden hazards such as wire.

On the approach to any fence, the horse must be balanced and in rhythm with plenty of impulsion. The more difficult the fence, the more impulsion is required. The rider must use his seat and legs strongly, resorting to the use of spurs and a whip as extra aids if the horse is reluctant to go forward. The rider should sit up, holding and driving the horse all the way to the fence. He must not drop the contract, nor lean forward until the horse has taken off.

If the horse quickens or lengthens his stride before a fence, he is likely to fall on to his forehand and lose balance. He will then be unable to adjust his stride, if necessary, for take-off. Just as in show jumping, it is important for a horse to be able to jump athletically.

Initially the speed should be a little faster than a good show-jumping pace. Rhythm and balance can then be established. Once the horse and rider become more experienced and competent, they can begin to aim for quicker times across country. Always remember that a few time penalties are preferable to jumping penalties. Time penalties will not prevent you from winning, but jumping errors will and may cause injury to horse and rider.

The rider must be able to adopt a 'safety seat' over a fence. This means sliding his seat back, keeping his head up, and pushing his weight forward against the stirrup as the horse lands. He must also be prepared to allow the reins to slip through his fingers. This safety seat is only possible if the rider is in balance, and he will find this easier to achieve if his stirrups are two or three holes shorter than his normal hacking length. It is vital to adopt the safety seat over a drop fence or if the horse makes a mistake.

A determined, positive attitude is crucial. If the horse thinks that you have doubts about a fence, he will soon lose heart.

Do seek the advice of an expert and learn to ride cross-country fences correctly. As with every sport, the more proficient you are, the more enjoyable it becomes and the less chance there is of injury.

Tack and equipment

Jumping at speed puts extra strain on leather and equipment, so good-quality tack, correctly fitted, is a must for any cross-country riding, be it schooling or taking part in a competition.

A jumping saddle which fits both horse and rider should be used with a well-fitting, securely fastened numnah. The girth must be strong with no signs of wear; and a surcingle should be worn when jumping to provide extra security. A breastplate or breastgirth is advisable to help keep the saddle in place.

Rubber reins give the most grip, especially when the reins become wet.

A running martingale provides both extra control and a useful neckstrap. Make sure that rein stops are used.

For safety, stirrup irons must be made of stainless steel and should be the correct size. Stirrup leathers should be made of rawhide because this will stretch

not break.

The horse's legs need protection against injury, either from hitting a fence or from one leg striking into another. The front legs are the most vulnerable. Leather tendon boots do not absorb water and there is no danger of them coming undone. Leg bandages should always be fitted by someone experienced. They must be applied with even pressure, then taped and sewn to keep them securely in place. Overreach boots must not be too large or the horse could tread on them and trip himself up.

Studs should be used when the going is slippery. Remember that front studs can be dangerous if the horse treads on you in the event of a fall.

At high-level competitions the front of the horse's legs are greased to help him 'slide' out of trouble over a fence. Never let any grease get on to the reins.

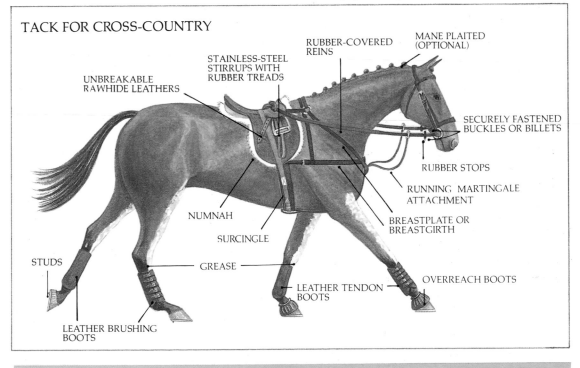

TACK FOR CROSS-COUNTRY

RUBBER-COVERED REINS

MANE PLAITED (OPTIONAL)

STAINLESS-STEEL STIRRUPS WITH RUBBER TREADS

UNBREAKABLE RAWHIDE LEATHERS

SECURELY FASTENED BUCKLES OR BILLETS

RUBBER STOPS

RUNNING MARTINGALE ATTACHMENT

NUMNAH

SURCINGLE

BREASTPLATE OR BREASTGIRTH

STUDS

GREASE

LEATHER TENDON BOOTS

OVERREACH BOOTS

LEATHER BRUSHING BOOTS

Rider's protection and safety

It is essential that the rider is correctly dressed for schooling or competition. Comfort and safety are both important. A well-fitting **crash cap** is *vital*. Any good saddler will advise on the correct fitting. A brightly coloured **silk** helps identify you on the course. Always wear a **body protector** and ensure that it is long enough to cover the base of the spine. It is sensible to wear **long sleeves** to protect your arms. A **hunting tie** gives support to the neck. The type of **gloves** you choose to wear depends on the weather but ensure that they give plenty of grip even when the reins or horse's neck are wet or sweaty.

Never jump in anything other than **correct footwear**.

If you wear glasses they must be special sports ones made of plastic. Remove all jewellery.

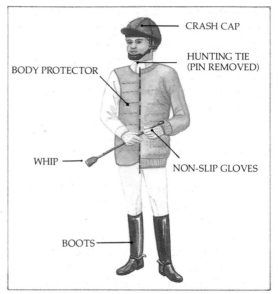

Essential clothing for safety. The artificial aids of a whip and spurs can be used to back up the rider's aids to ensure that the horse always goes forward.

Walking the course

At cross-country competitions the rider has the opportunity to examine the course and its fences, and to study the take-offs and landings at each obstacle. He should decide exactly how and where to jump each fence and memorise his route ('line') into and away from the jumps. Uneconomical routes waste time.

The distances between elements of combination fences can be paced out and a riding plan decided.

It is important to note how each fence strikes on first impression. This is how the horse will see the fences, so the rider must decide how to approach each one and give his horse clear messages.

The rider should take note of the going and how it may change. He should also take care to count the fence numbers en route and watch for any turning flags.

Allow plenty of time to walk the course and commit the details to memory.

The start and the first fence

Before the horse can be expected to put up a good cross-country performance, he must be properly warmed-up. He can then be quietly walked round at the start until called to the start box. Make sure that he is alert but try to avoid making him over-excited.

As soon as the starter says 'Go!' ride positively towards the first fence, and try to establish a rhythm as soon as possible. Bear in mind that the horse is leaving 'home' and may be rather reluctant. He may need riding more strongly than normal until he is properly underway. Make sure that the approach is absolutely straight and that the horse knows which way he is expected to go. Do not allow him to wander into the fence; instead encourage him to attack it enthusiastically but without either losing rhythm or increasing speed. If he hangs badly towards home or the horseboxes he may need a kick or even a smart tap with the whip to remind him of his job. The horse must learn to be forward-thinking if he is to be a good cross-country performer.

Good jumps over the first few fences lay the foundations of a confident clear round. If the horse jumps the early fences rather stickily and without enthusiasm it implies that the rest of the round may be the same. If the horse does not jump the first fence well, a tap with the whip on landing will sharpen him up.

Although the first fence is always straightforward it is important that the horse jumps it correctly and does not flatten over it. He must be made to bascule (jump in a round shape) over it so that he is prepared for any more demanding obstacles that he may encounter.

Steeplechase fence

This is the most inviting of all fences and is often found on a cross-country course. The steeplechase element of a three-day event (Phase B) has eight to ten fences to be negotiated at a gallop. The horse must jump them out of his stride and rhythm so that he takes the least out of himself.

Although an easy fence, the rider must ensure that the horse jumps it without flattening too much. Always remember that the fences which follow may well be athletically demanding, and if the horse has jumped a fence fast and flat, he may find it difficult to adjust suddenly to jumping in a round shape.

By all means 'keep coming' over this type of fence. There is no need to 'set up' (i.e. slow down and gather the horse together) too much, but try not to accelerate on the approach, which is a common fault.

Steeplechase fence – one of the most inviting fences. This rider has adopted a good safety seat.

Ditch away

Any fence with a ditch on the landing side presents a hidden hazard. Having walked the course, the rider is aware of the ditch but the horse is not. It is up to the rider to explain to his horse that he must jump well out over the fence.

The rider must approach strongly, creating plenty of impulsion, but keeping the horse balanced and in rhythm, and not allowing him to fall on to his forehand. The approach must be positive and attacking with enough pace to carry the horse over the ditch on landing. The rider must make sure that he stays in position and uses the stirrup as a brace, just in case the horse pecks on landing by dropping a leg in the ditch. With this sort of fence the rider must be prepared to adopt the safety seat (see page 4).

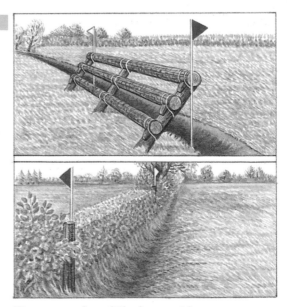

Two examples of 'ditch away' fences: *top* – elephant trap; *above* – natural hedge with a ditch.

Triple bar

This is another straightforward, inviting fence. There is no need to 'set up' too much, but do maintain rhythm, balance and impulsion. It is important not to stand off too far at a triple bar because this makes the jump very wide and there is a danger of the horse hitting the back rail.

On the approach the rider should ride the horse strongly into his hand so that the horse has his hocks well under him and has lightened his forehand ready for the jump. If his hocks are engaged he is less likely to make a flat jump or 'dive' over the fence.

Any sloping spread fence should be approached in the same way. Engage the horse a dozen or so strides away, then keep hold and keep riding.

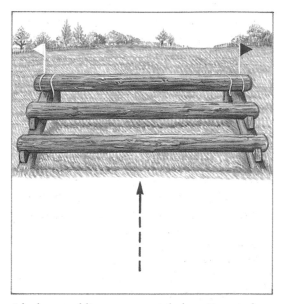

Ideal central line over a triple bar. Remember that a show jump will knock down but a cross-country fence is unforgiving.

Sharks' teeth

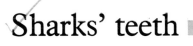

When tackling a sharks' teeth the line of approach is the most important aspect. The horse has to be confident about where he is expected to take off and must not be in danger of putting his feet on the fence itself. The best place for which to aim is in between the 'teeth' and there is normally a most central point, bearing in mind that the best line over a fence is in the middle. The Vs of the teeth act as wings to keep the horse straight and encourage him to look what he is doing.

Horses normally jump this type of fence well, provided that the rider approaches correctly.

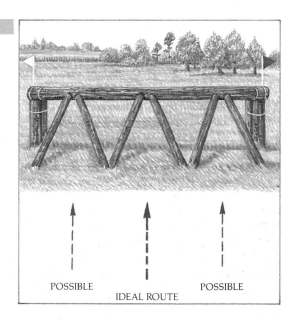

Options over sharks' teeth.

Trakehner

A trakehner is a ditch with either a rail or a tree trunk above it. This rail or log can be in a variety of positions. The standard trakehner has the rail/log centrally over the ditch, but it can be set at an angle or closer to the front or the back of the ditch.

When the rail is central, the ditch in front provides a good groundline. As long as the horse has no aversions to ditches, this should prove a straightforward and inviting fence to jump. The rider needs to ride strongly, however, and should not be intimidated by the ditch. Whilst riding strongly, he must on no account let the horse fall on to his forehand and lose balance. He must first drive the horse together, then keep riding and at the same time hold the front end.

When the rail or log is angled, the line to choose is one where the ditch provides a groundline and there is not too much ditch on the landing side. Jump the ditch at right angles with the rail at an angle because this is easier for the horse to decide where to take off.

If the log is situated towards the front of the ditch, the fence has to be treated as an upright and the horse needs to be 'set up' for it. If the log is on the far side, it places more demands on the horse's courage. If the horse is slightly timid about jumping over ditches, it is important for the rider to have plenty of energy in his hand, with the horse's hocks even further underneath him on the approach. In this way, the rider can keep the horse's head up and not allow him to drop on to his forehand and look down into the ditch.

Jumping these fences well is all about confidence of both horse and rider.

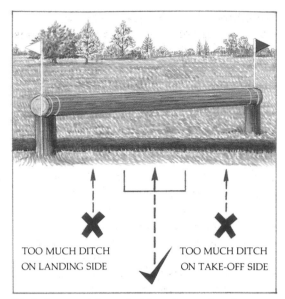

Trakehner with angled log. Jump this fence at right angles to the ditch, leaving enough ditch for a groundline.

Deviating from the golden rule of always jumping the middle of a fence can sometimes make the obstacle more inviting, as shown here.

Bullfinch

A bullfinch is a tall hedge with high wispy twigs through which the horse has to jump. These may be quite thick, making the fence seem like an impenetrable barrier. The horse has to be brave and barge his way through the top half of the fence. Unless the rider explains, by very strong riding, that the fence must be jumped, the horse may well question the wisdom of attempting such a fearsome-looking object! The horse must trust and obey his rider.

The line of approach must be absolutely straight. The horse must be full of impulsion and ready to tackle the fence positively. The rider must sit up, keep hold and keep driving until the moment of take-off in case the horse hesitates.

Bullfinches test the horse's courage and trust in his rider. Make sure he knows that you mean him to jump through it.

Open ditch

A fence with a ditch in front is called an open ditch. A cross-country open ditch may feature a hedge, rails, pallisade or any other solid obstacle. (It becomes a trakehner if the fence itself is not solid.) These fences can be intimidating for the rider, particularly if he lacks experience or confidence. A ditch in front of a fence acts as a take-off rail and in fact makes the fence easier for the horse to judge his take-off point. It also makes the jump itself easier by making the horse 'back off' and so not get too close to the fence for take-off. Ride strongly to the fence, keeping hold and maintaining the rhythm, balance and impulsion.

A ditch in front of a fence gives the horse a good groundline from which to take off. Riders lacking in experience or confidence may find these fences off-putting.

Coffin

A coffin is one of the most influential fences on a cross-country course. It consists of a ditch with a fence on either side. This fence may comprise rails or logs or even a pallisade. The distances between the obstacles and the ditch may vary from a bounce to one or two strides.

A half coffin is a single fence with a ditch; a double coffin has two ditches in between the fences. Again, the distances between the two ditches may vary.

Most courses have a coffin and since they create so much trouble, it is well worth spending time schooling over a variety of coffins at home before attempting to tackle them in competitions. As with any fence which differs from the straightforward, confidence is all-important. When training, the horse must firstly be happy about ditches on their own. He should then progress to popping over a small rail

in conjunction with a ditch, and then finally he can attempt all three elements.

The approach is the crucial factor in negotiating a coffin successfully. The horse must arrive in a bouncy canter, with his hocks well engaged; he must be light on his forehand, in balance and in rhythm. The 'revs' should be high but the pace controlled. If the horse is long and fast in the approach, he will be encouraged to jump with a flat, shallow parabola. If he jumps the first element too boldly, he may well land in the ditch itself.

A coffin can be rather spooky and the ditch may take the horse by surprise. The rider must therefore be very strong and determined in his riding, keeping the horse short, bouncy and full of energy.

Remember to keep riding all the way through the coffin rather than just concentrating on the first part.

Good secure seat, head up, heels down.

Danger of rider losing balance if horse spooks at the ditch.

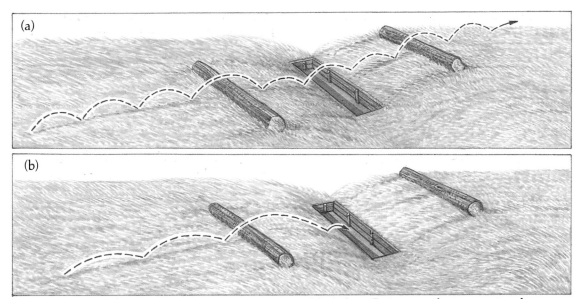

(a) An approach with a short, bouncy canter makes the coffin easy for the horse.

(b) A fast, flat approach encourages the horse to jump so big that he is in danger of landing in the ditch itself. This will frighten him and make him worry in the future.

If the rider's body is too far forward he is in front of the movement. Rider must stay 'behind' the horse until he takes off over the final element.

Water fences

Riding strongly in a short, bouncy canter

Horse sees water and hesitates – possible refusal ahead – but rider keeps hold, sits up and continues to ride strongly

Successful jump into water

Horses have a natural fear of water. They must have implicit trust in their rider if they are to jump into water because they have no idea of the depth. This trust takes time to build up but can be destroyed very quickly if the horse is presented badly at a water fence and is given a fright.

All the horse's energy must be gathered on the approach so that he arrives at the fence in a short, bouncy canter with maximum impulsion. The rider must drive strongly without allowing the horse to lengthen. He should keep his body upright, staying 'behind' the horse.

If the horse jumps in too fast he might lose his balance on landing due to the drag of the water. Once in the water the rider must use his legs, while maintaining a contact to preserve energy and balance. When in water, it is better not to change pace because this uses valuable energy and disturbs the equilibrium.

If there is a fence in the water itself, do not allow the horse to fall on to his forehand as he approaches. Instead keep driving and keep hold all the way to the fence. On no account drop the contact: the horse must be 'between hand and leg'.

The same applies to jumping out of water. It requires a lot of effort for a horse to jump out of water and he needs help. The rider must keep his weight back to help lighten the horse's forehand before take-off but be ready to swing forward and give with his hand when the horse jumps. Sometimes it is difficult to stay with the horse. This is why so much emphasis is put on the rider's position and balance.

Fences in water need positive riding. The horse must be between hand and leg.

Open water or ditch

The horse has to realise that he has to make one big jump and clear the whole expanse of water or jump the ditch from bank to bank. In some instances, the horse has to jump into water, yet at other times he is expected to jump over it and not land in it. It is therefore the rider's task to convey, positively and clearly, what is wanted. Any diffidence on the rider's behalf will confuse the horse and make him indecisive. This is when a problem is likely to occur. If the rider's message is loud and clear, the horse should respond accordingly.

To encourage the horse to take a big leap, the rider must ride strongly on the approach and keep a good pace without going too fast. The horse must be pushed up together from behind to engage his hocks, keeping him in rhythm and balance; the impulsion must be maintained all the way to the fence. The horse must have a chance to see where he is to take off and land. If the rider allows the horse to gallop headlong into a ditch or open water, the horse may plunge straight in, not realising that he has to jump over it. By setting up the horse, shifting his balance back on to his hocks, the rider is giving a clear indication that the horse must jump and make an effort.

If the edges of a ditch are not well defined, it is necessary to trot or even walk the last few strides. The horse can then feel his way to the take-off point. If the ditch is very large, the horse may have to creep down one side before jumping to the other bank, or halfway up it. The rider must decide how best to approach and negotiate the ditch before he attempts to jump it.

Wide water jumps must be cleared in a large leap, so the horse needs a strong message that he must jump over and not into the water.

A wide ditch with sloping sides can be negotiated by allowing the horse to creep down one side before jumping across.

Steps and banks

Steps and banks are a test of a horse's
power and agility. He must jump from
his hocks, which means he must be light
on his forehand in the approach and full
of impulsion. It is essential to establish a
short, bouncy canter, making sure that
the line of approach is absolutely straight.
With a series of steps, the horse is liable
to lose impulsion on the way up, so the
rider must keep hold and keep riding to
the very top. It is easy to jump the first
step and sit complacently, only to be
rewarded with a refusal.

Steps down should be approached at a
bouncy trot.

Banks must be tackled in much the
same way as steps. If the pace is too fast,
the horse may stumble.

The rider must keep riding all the way
over a bank. He must keep his balance
slightly 'behind' the horse when on the
top of a bank to avoid jumping off alone!

If an Irish bank is approached too fast, the
horse may not have time to find his footing
and could stumble. He needs to gather his
energy and spring on to the slope.

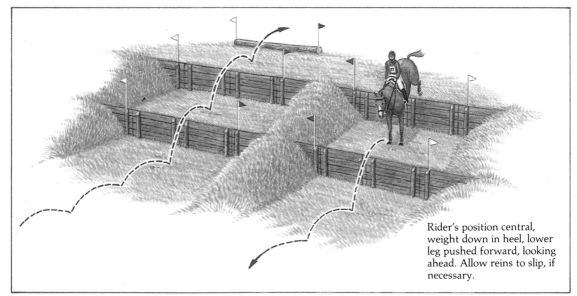

Rider's position central,
weight down in heel, lower
leg pushed forward, looking
ahead. Allow reins to slip, if
necessary.

Steps up require that the horse jumps from
his hocks, so he must have plenty of
impulsion. Keep riding positively, right up to
the top step.

Steps down should be approached from a
bouncy canter to a bouncy trot, without
losing impulsion. The rider must keep riding
forward.

Sunken road

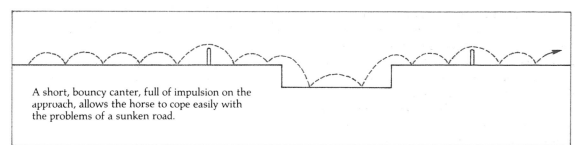

A short, bouncy canter, full of impulsion on the approach, allows the horse to cope easily with the problems of a sunken road.

This demands courage, agility and discipline and, like a coffin, can cause a fair amount of trouble on a cross-country course. It should not, however, cause a problem if the horse is happy with steps and knows how to use himself athletically.

The correct approach is essential if the horse is to jump through easily. The horse needs the same bouncy canter – i.e. full of energy, with balance and rhythm – that other difficult fences demand.

Strong, positive riding is essential, with the horse's energy contained all the way to take-off. This, coupled with the horse's trust in his rider, means that the horse should pop through without any trouble.

Problems occur when the pace is too fast or when the horse is unbalanced and without impulsion. It is important that the line chosen is straight and that the horse can see where he is going.

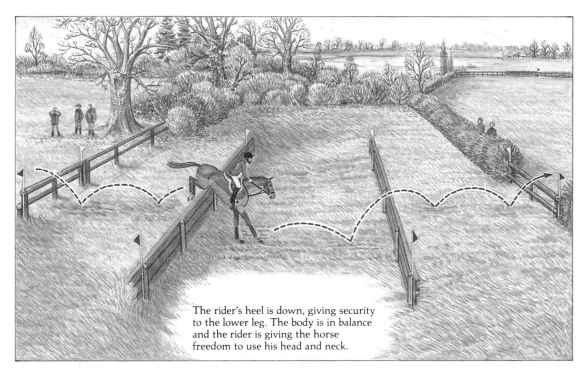

The rider's heel is down, giving security to the lower leg. The body is in balance and the rider is giving the horse freedom to use his head and neck.

Drop fence

The horse will be unaware that a drop lurks on the landing side of this fence, but the rider, however, will have noted its existence during his course walk.

All drop fences must be respected. The horse can easily lose his balance when he lands because the drop takes him by surprise. The rider must be prepared for this with his weight pushed forward on the stirrup, his head up and his fingers ready to slip the reins.

On the approach, the horse must be well balanced with his weight on his hocks, not on his forehand. The rider must sit up well.

Riding a drop off a ledge is rather like riding a big step. The horse must be kept coming forward in a bouncy trot – he will automatically slow down. If he stops and hesitates, the rider must be ready to drive him forward to avoid a refusal.

Three examples of a drop fence.

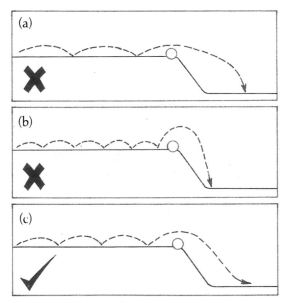

Approach: (a) too flat and fast; (b) too short and slow – jump too steep; (c) medium pace and stride – the most comfortable way to jump.

Hayrack with a false groundline

If a fence does not have a clear take-off rail, it is difficult for a horse to judge his take-off point. The horse looks at the base of the fence to see where he should take off, and if this line is directly under, or even behind the front rail of the fence, it will encourage the horse to run in too close to the fence. As a result the horse will probably hit the fence and, if the pace is fast, this may well cause the horse to fall. It is necessary for the rider to help his horse by 'setting him up' beforehand so that the pace is reduced and the horse is well off his forehand with his hocks underneath him. During this time of adjustment, the rider must ensure that the horse remains in rhythm and does not lose impulsion. The rider must sit up well on the approach to help keep the horse's weight off his forehand.

Shadow causing false groundline.

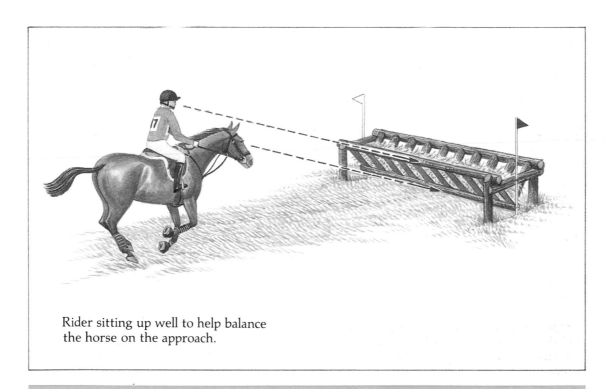

Rider sitting up well to help balance the horse on the approach.

Combination fences

These vary from having one stride to three or even four strides in between elements, and can be a combination of any type of obstacle. These fences require careful walking and every option should be examined. The rider must know which alternative route to take, should his first choice prove a problem. He should know exactly where to go if his horse refuses at any one part. The rider has to choose the route that will best suit his horse. Experience and ability must be taken into account. The risk involved in jumping the most difficult route must be weighed against the amount of time that it saves. Sometimes it is better to take a slightly slower, easier route. The distances between elements may influence the decision. A short-striding horse will cope more easily with a short distance than a long-striding horse. A long-distance may make a small horse struggle.

The horse must arrive balanced, in rhythm and with impulsion. He must come in absolutely straight and with no doubt in his mind about which way he is to go. Any hesitation from the rider will immediately be transferred to the horse.

To help find the right line it is useful to use landmarks.

Combination fences should not be approached fast or the horse may land too far out over the first element. This will make the distance to the next element too short and the horse may have a problem at the second part. If the distance between elements measures the same as a show-jumping distance, then the rider should know the pace required.

Combination fences call for precision riding and accuracy. They need concentration on the course walk and when ridden.

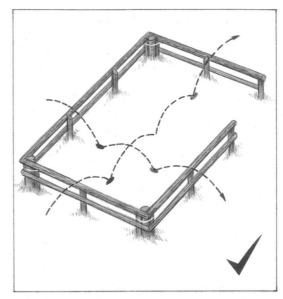

An even rhythm gives an even stride.

Landing point   Take-off point

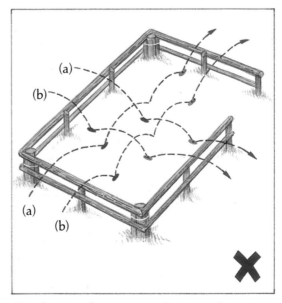

Landing too far in or not far enough causes problems at the second element. (a) Too close for take-off. (b) Too far off for take-off.

Bounce fence

The fence name indicates the type of approach necessary for a successful jump. The horse has to be agile and athletic to bounce (i.e. jump two or more elements without taking a stride in between). The distance in a bounce may vary from 11ft (3.5m) to 18ft (5.5m) depending on whether the course is for ponies or horses. The shorter the distance, the more agile the horse has to be, and the approach more bouncy and controlled. The rider must gather the horse together on the approach. The horse must be well balanced, on his hocks, and in a rhythmical, bouncy canter. He can then literally 'bounce' through the combination. The rider must stay in balance, *keeping a contact throughout* so that the horse is helped to spring immediately into the air on landing.

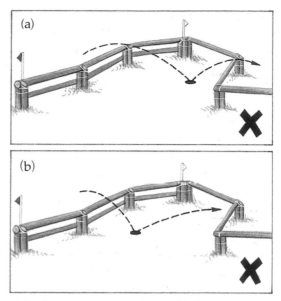

(a) The jump in is too long; (b) the jump in is too short.

● Landing and take-off point

Corner

A corner requires more precision riding than any other fence. It demands accuracy and obedience and should not be attempted until both horse and rider are experienced. Any misjudgment will result in a run-out, a fall or a bad experience, all of which will jeopardise future confidence.

The approach and line to the fence are all-important. The approach must have the right pace, with rhythm, balance and impulsion. The line must be exactly to the point of take-off.

In order to decide where to jump a corner, divide the angle of the corner in half and aim for an imaginary line in between the front and back rail. Depending on the width of the rails, the line should be as near to the point of the corner as possible without the risk of the horse running out. There is no room for error.

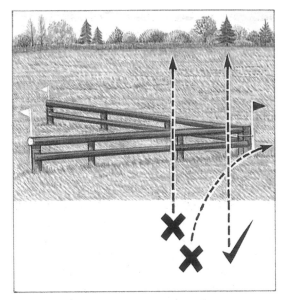

Approaching a corner. Many riders use a distant landmark to help them find the line.

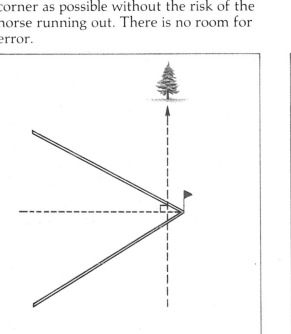

Dissect the angle to find the centre line and jump at right angles to it.

Trees and darkness are possible distractions that can cause a horse to run out (to the left in the above situation). Ride accurately.

Jumping into darkness

Jumping a fence into darkness, say on the edge of a wood, can be rather menacing; leaving the bright light and possibly turning away from home is uninviting. A fence whose landing is in darkness becomes doubly difficult if it includes a ditch or a drop.

It is important that the line into the fence is completely straight and that the horse is given ample time to adjust his eyes to the dark. The rider must sit up, gather the energy and then ride very positively into the fence. The pace should be full of impulsion but not too fast. The faster the pace, the greater the element of surprise and the more reason the horse has for stopping. Any change of light should be noted when walking the course, as should how the sun might affect a fence.

A fence with a roof will have the same threatening affect as darkness.

A fence under a roof can appear menacing to a horse.

This simple log fence is made more difficult than it looks because the horse has to jump it from light into dark.

Another straightforward fence whose landing side plunges horse and rider into relative darkness. If approached too fast the element of surprise is even greater.

Final thoughts

- The old adage, 'Throw your heart over the fence and your horse will follow!' does not work.

- **Keep hold** and **keep driving** but **wait for the fence to come to you**.

- **Approach every fence straight** and **jump it in the middle** if possible.

- Walk the course carefully and concentrate on **lines**, **turns**, the **going** and **alternatives**.

- **Use landmarks** to help hold the correct lines into fences, but choose distinctive reference points – one tree can look very like another.

- A fast time is not achieved by going flat out but by riding **accurate, economical lines**.

- It is not the speed at which the horse jumps the fence that is important but the **speed by which he is back in his rhythm**.

- **Impulsion not speed**, however difficult the fence.

- If a fence is very difficult, imagine that the horse has already stopped once so you need to **ride with more determination**.

- Keep your **heels** and your **hands down**, and your **head up** – especially over drop fences.